innerfruit

Erin Crowley

VITALITY
buzz, bliss + books

innerfruit: rhymes of growing pains and vibrant awakenings
Copyright © 2024 by Erin Crowley

Published by VITALITY buzz, bliss + books LLC
vitalitybuzz.org

Proceeds from sales of this book benefit the mission of VITALITY Cincinnati Inc: transforming lives through holistic self-care from neighborhood to neighborhood, person to person, and breath by breath since 2010. It's the power of the circle!

Every effort has been made to give credit to other people's original ideas within the text. If you feel something should be credited to someone and is not, please get in touch through our website and every effort will be made to correct this text for future printings. Thank you!

We invite you to honor your mind, your body, your whole self. Do only what you know to be right for you. While the invitations offered here in this book, on our websites and social media, and in our classes are geared to be gentle and easily modified by the participant to fit the participants' needs, please consult your medical doctor or health professional before undertaking any practices.

ISBN: 978-1-954688-21-6
Library of Congress Control Number: applied for

In gratitude to our VATRONS
who seek with us all a new way forward &
who have helped bring forward this new volume
by pre-ordering their copy — we thank you!

Hana Rosalie Alleva, Lynn Alley, Eva Atrano, Alex Braun,
Iona Crowley, Terri Crowley, Dave Eby, Courtney Gentile,
Zack Gustat, Joseph Hoodin, Kristopher Kelley, Vernita Leins,
Adam Merchant, Lucas Merker, Zara Misler, Diana L. Newman,
Bridget Omalley, Cassidy Padgett, Melissa Rowland, Nick Sawyer,
Alora Seitz, Brian Shircliff, Juniper Stromer, Adrianna Tilton,
Katie Todd, Zef Vesel, Christine Whelan, Dawn Woodward,
Carrie Woodward, Casey Worth, Carol Yeazell

AUM: The everywhere vibrational force. The binding between matter beholding intelligence and power that is the source of all creation everyday. The "invisible" field or for some "in-visible" field of sparkling, flickering love particles glimpsed in the field of vision. The scent of roses in your nose. The creative aliveness of the air all around us always. In the ether, in the medium, we find Creative Source Energy all around us waiting for us to engage. The space between, the flickering love particles, the infinite bliss, love and fearlessness.

CONTENTS

introduction

This is a book of surrender. A compilation of experiences requesting gracious surrender over and over again. Surrender of expectation. Surrender of past limiting beliefs. A surrender to placing the feet so graciously on the ground. A called surrender for the longing of lost love. A chosen surrender of resistance to the path. Surrender sometimes met only when the self is so incredibly exhausted that it just feels good to let go.

Along the path, along *your* path, this book is a testament to honor you. To honor you for embarking on *your path* of healing. To honor your humility of experience when challenges arise. To honor your heart for opening and feeling into the deepest aches of suppression. To honor your unending commitment to growing your *innermost* self. I honor you for your courage and I honor you for your fears. For we are in this together, this is why we are here.

When you read through this book, I wish for you to take what you feel as *your knowing*. I wish for you to hold a little bit of extra space for the notions and even resistances that may surface inside. I wish for you to notice them. I wish for you to feel them without an obligation to label them as yours. I wish for you to feel, then, I wish you let them go. I most wish for you to trust that where your attention goes mid-sentence is where it is significant to notice. Notice what bubbles up inside so that it can continue upward, into the seen, known and ever onward. When you see what is bubbling up, it can bubble up all the way and suddenly "bloop!" Sweet release and integration rather than seated in resistance amid indigestion. Let them pass. Whether yours, mine or theirs; whether pleasant, grim or indifferent; none are yours to keep forever nor would you prefer they forever stay. We need not touch, hold or keep to remember.

There are 12 phases (or chapters) in this book and not a linear flow do they follow. Though numerically aligned, the eras of self-realization come and you experience them. You do what you will and move into a phase most suited for your ascension. There are no hinges between the doors of progress. You may jump around - back and forth - revisiting scenes both familiar and obscure. Perhaps, a feeling you've been there before. You may surface ahead and glimpse an understanding you had not known you were ready for. You may take away insights from both the paths "behind" and the paths seeming "advanced," and again, find a centering back into your perfect medium of progress.

Sometimes you may feel you have worked longer and harder in this chapter than any other. Sometimes you stop to smell the flowers of the path you are on because it flew by in the blink of an eye. Sometimes a theme of achievement will flow over you and *your truth* tells you, "you've come far." You've secured a divine lesson. Then, you find next a reintroduction to familiar details skimmed over beholding more significance than you could see in the light of that day. A lesson to try a different hand with. A lesson to try again. And you move, you just stay in motion. Though there may be times of seeming stagnation, I invite you to remember the feeling of first learning the Earth is always spinning. A child so graciously gravitated to the path; awareness comes as a focal point, from alone time and less from the mass.

Pay less mind to the order of the chapters numbered here, it is merely one outcome of infinite potentials for experience. And if it were possible for you imagine the chapters of this book printed in a multifaceted, layered kind-of-way, you would see the boundless multitude of chapters there could be to experience. Infinitive varieties. Articulately designed. And aligned. For the comprehension of the experiencer. Organization dependent on your choosing, on your schooling, on cycles of learning, practicing and growing.

I do wish to tell you how *loved* you are. You are as significant as the Sun in the sky. Of the highest power is your parallel importance. The sparkle in your eye, the spontaneous smile you do not see, the flushing of your cheeks and the *light* you shine. I love to see, feel and adore these raw beauties of you that you do not see. Behind the eyes that glimmer is *you*.

Part in the self-conscious mind you reside. Part of you residing in *being* glimpses this side I see of you; perhaps, the *body* of you provides a reminder. Abundance surrounds you, dances around you - entices you to choose empowerment. Vastness more wide than ever dreamed on the "planet of choice."

You are so sacred, child, beheld in the weaving of existence. Interconnected, so deeply loved and in regard for, at all times along your path - you are always connected to an immeasurable supply of *loving light*. Whether you shine your light that day or you keep it inside to warm you up, you are *safe*. You are together - with me and with *all*; you are taken care of. You are *whole*. There is none missing from you. All that you seek is yours - available to you at all times and you will find inside. You are loved. Oh child, you are so loved and taken care of.

When you are feeling bright - radiate and shine. I wish you the courage to stand up and feel most *alive* in sharing your *light* with the world. To hold back for caution of outshining another brings two flames to smolder. To rise and ignite your embodiment of truth gives rise to other fires in need of spark. Quickly they fill the spaces between you with their returned, wild and inspired flame. When *unconditional love* lights the way - change, healing and growth escalate. When together we bind in a shared path of self-discovery, the collective path accelerates. Together. We are home. We come to remember our sameness.

Boundaries dissolve in the *heart* of mutual understanding. Together, in *oneness*, we find a way to comfort in a moment a thousand years of pain. The aches break and we become *safe* again - knowing we have all felt alone. Isn't that what we all seek? To find the path back *hOMe*? To be courageous enough to follow the path in love and light and grace and peace? To listen to the *guiding compass*? In utter acceptance of the terrifyingly tangible, infinitive nature of the universe?

Let us be easy on ourselves and others. Let us be gentle. Let us smell the roses. Let us lift each other up. Let us lift ourselves. In love. Love, love, love.

And *love*.

1

Preparing the Seeds

The preparation of journey in the soul's quest for healing. The catalysts for growth seeded in interconnected and coincidental experiences. The alignment of opportunity as self begins to go inward and open.

Sitting Still
Seemingly
SAS
Forest of Love
Ab-SPLACT
Remind
Gooey
Remember This Day
Retraction
Moreover
Egoistic Policy

Sitting Still

I sit
As I sit
I continue to knit
Together the words
The words in my head
They push and they shove
Confusing the stream
Less concrete than a dream
Transcendental
They seem

Seemingly

All things that are green
Impossible they seem
I feel the deity
It wells inside me
The things I had known
All slipped away
Instead, a fountain of
I n f i n i t y
Had taken
Its place

SAS

I feel every beat

drum · drum · drum

Inside me
It moves me
Everything that I have become
Everything I want - any special need
None of it matters
I've been set free
The room is bursting with joy
Something like I've never seen
We're all one
There is no in-between
Grateful thoughts fill my mind
Life has changed drastically
Without these people
I would have been lost

E·t·e·r·n·a·l·l·y

Forest of Love

The forest was wise,
a place of truth & magic
— combined —
I found peace, I felt love . . .
such a place had never existed
besides in my mind
The auras before us
sang like a chorus
but the melody of the song
was the *boy in the forest*
Eyes of the earth,
humble spirit — of a monk —
the second split, then, my heart sunk
It was here, it was now,
and then it was gone
like a still night's darkness,
just moments before dawn

We followed different paths,
but more similar than we knew
and then, I was stilled
waiting for the storm to brew
a n n n d . . .

It rained laughter,
it poured genuine necessity
when the skies had cleared,
the *boy in the forest* was now a part of me
Blinded by perfection of his every flawless trait,
it had now occurred to me . . .
The *boy in the forest*,
was not a minute late

Ab-SPLACT

Boxes upon the wall; SPLAT
they expand, they contract
Nobody sees the boxes, but me,
though the wall may seem to be;
the boxes are hardly compact
They turn into lines and down they fall
and there I sit
and I sat

A story is told, a message unfolds
They sling, and they slung,
and they SPLAT

The wave crashes
an aura of blue intensity
It hadn't been too many blinks ago,
when the boxes asked a dance of me
Could it be? OH. Could it be?

PANCAKE

Splat

GOBLIN

Attack

WILLOWS UNITE

[they put up a fight

Bazinga

Eureka

A b s t r a c t ——

I DOUGHNUT FEEL
I DOUGHNUT FEEL
I DOUGHNUT FEEL

et all.

I WALNUT FEEL
I WALNUT FEEL
I WALNUT FEEL

fortune.

Remind

An illusion, I feel
Solid it seems
Clouds of darkness
As insecurity deems
Arisen I've become
A string upon my temple
I've been given new eyes
No less than ample
False claims fade
Accusations subside
Shame on you
Inner voice
That lied

Gooey

A poem or two
A poem for you
Your soul
It sings
Melodic danger
And happiness
It brings
You & me
Like rubber & glue
You bounce me around the room
And suddenly
I'm stuck
To an allegory found inside you
I've never seen eyes
More true

Remember This Day

Sometimes it's not easy
to remember what we have
to praise the gift of life
to forget about being mad
Sometimes it's not clear
that the forces have a plan
that we've not come up short
that we're so much more than man
Sometimes we're unsure
and today that's okay
and tomorrow too, they say
one day we'll find a better way
Until then, just play

Retraction

Make me remember
Force me to recall
Alone we are never
Together we fall
Incredible it is
To disconnect from the mass
When intertwined, we are,
Though the faces, they pass
Superficially bound
Taken by the rift
Better to root in the ground
When cosmically adrift
Dig, dig, dig deep inside
Latch onto the core
Don't set the bar too high
The most stable is the floor
Retract and you'll find
A key to a door
Upon harvesting the courage
To inwardly explore

Moreover

This moment is pure, sacred, often forgotten
Overridden by distraction, ruled by attraction
Disillusioned by want, need be subjective
Molded by desire of the common collective
"I's" among "I's"
Your story is mine
Devised by perspective
Isolation is a lie
Your feelings are felt
A cup runneth over
To all is an impact
Not luck from a clover
Red rover, red rover...

Egoistic Policy

R E P U B L I C

?

To put the people in power
To elect our own hierarchy
Seemingly fair –> people of the heir
Or a dim and hidden possibility?

Does pride T R U M P peace?

Is human separate from human?
Approaching an atomic disaster

Who is the T R U M A N ?

Ego feeds upon violence
and soul upon love

With motionless yin among innovative yang
Balance will steep when push comes to shove

2

Breaking Through

The growing pains and shaking heartache following soul's acceptance of the path. The sudden, unexpected breakthroughs and ecstatic moments of bliss in beginning. The inner-fruiting curiosity and awareness of energetic interconnection. The inherent knowingness of realms far beyond our own.

Metamorphic Thoughts
Darkness
Wholey
Growing Pains
Inner Ground
Death By Love
Stay
A Controlled Bloomer
Difficult Horizons
A Fearful Foundation
Swimming Lessons
Treading Water
Soul Surfing
A Breath Of Self

Metamorphic Thoughts

It flows, in and out, of my soul
A moment of metamorphosis
Enlightenment
A |small part| of the whole
Energy abides concurrent to thought
You'll soon be reminded

of what you forgot

L i f e   s t a n d s   s t i l l . . .

Darkness

You were my rock;
my stability, my virtue
Always me who needed help;
it was never you
A new found wall between us;
and then, you were gone
It's like throwing a rock into the *darkness*
There was no response
"How can I help?
What can I do?"

"Nothing, I'm going to sleep;
and you should too."

Wholey

The bounds of my body tremble
Your eyes hypnotize my soul
I've waited all my life for acceptance
Of the longing
The craving I cannot control
My world is sent spinning
And again
I am left perplexed
Are we existing in the same reality?
Or did I mistake a small part
For the wh0le . . .

Growing Pains

He stole the heart from her sleeve,
placing a tear in her eye for exchange
It hardened her heart,
it darkened her soul

She couldn't help but feel estranged

Sometime within the healing,
a soft voice was noticed inside
Familiar in tone, as firm as a stone —
the sensation of being Alive

The dawning of a new day accompanied by a dream,
brought peace to her soul, making her whole,
never experiencing a change so extreme

What you think, you become,
and what you become is you
She found herself that day,
he'd never seen her colors so true

Her world was coming together
as if magnetized by her spirit
She had opened her mind, freed her soul —
and now everyone could see it

They came running, beckoning for compassion
to mend the hearts of resentment
But now she had found a kindred soul,
one who brought her contentment

Opportunities will come, and in time,
they shall pass
Be conscious of each decision
see things for what they are

Happiness shall come
at last

Inner Ground

In a trance, I stand
Lost within you
Every last layer,
I know you see through
Searching to find a firmer ground,
though a piece deep inside —
I seem to have found
How astound

Death By Love

Eyes that caution me as wild,
tempting with mystery,
an aura of a child
Impulsive, elusive, and
impermanent at best
Your colors are rare —
resonating in my chest,
standing afar the rest,
posing the ultimate test

cardiac arrest

Stay

I am not me
My bounds do not exist
I am eager to be set free
Sensations of a forbidden kiss
I am not me
I am you, and him, and her,
and t h e m
I cannot flee,
for it is of the same root,
that one and all stem
I am not me
Unfamiliar courage from far beyond
With closed eyes, I can see,
A magnificent morning; just dawned
I am not me
Layers shed as the skin of a snake
It's the shade beneath the tree,
revealed by light; a cognitive quake
I am not me
Nor should I choose to believe
Not simply organic debris
Yet, improbable to conceive
I am not me.
Hello, I am we.

A Controlled Bloomer

A symbol of a flower,
of late to bloom
Hidden away in the darkness,
though it's nearly noon
Is it dead?
Afraid?
Secluded by nature?
Cast away by choice?
An erotically aloof creature
A minuscule wake, a trembling petal,
a moment of vulnerability
– there's life –
So fearsome to settle
Exposure provides a path of return,
still, the beauty inside awaits
Until experienced,
one cannot learn
Overcoming the heart's
debate

Difficult Horizons

A million bands of rubber
Wrapped around my head
Tension like the war between
The walking and the living dead
Confusion as if a nap awoken
Amidst a dream – so real
Lost between my perception
And how you truly feel;
– Surreal –
Emotions locked inside a safe
The only trust I keep
Shattered by your eyes like glass
In a vulnerable oblivion;
– I weep –
Keep your assumptions to yourself
Hide your lies away
I've found the path among the trees
From my journey
I shall not stray

A Fearful Foundation

I feel darkness upon the fringe
though not a tangible terror
the fear of which makes me cringe
In this moment, all is not lost
but to reside in the future
How great is the cost?
Beautiful moments pass
opportunities fade as subtle
the passion once held
seems mixed with the rubble
To let go is the task
upon holding is danger
Consciousness streams too quickly
I've emerged as a stranger
Frantic cries, screams for salvation
Who am I? What am I?
Ambiguous Creation

Swimming Lessons

Holding back feelings
afraid of response
Like swimming upstream
drowning in thoughts
A river of confusion
only avoided together
But the fog has settled in
should've checked the weather
The distance is far
drifting from stable ground
Seems a moment ago
we were safe and sound
With no sense of direction
no compass nor map
Seems we've been here before

punished by another lap

Treading Water

It's been awhile
I'm certain
Caught up in the chaos
Wrapped up in the curtain
Hiding from the day
Strangled by the night
Begging for resolution
But too tired to fight
I can see the path ahead
But the journey is blurred
Self-medication falls short of a cure
Lost among faces and comfort be rare
Discontent; with more than a fair share
Snap out of it, quit doubting it
The whole world is in your hands

Let go,

Continue to flow

But first,

Establish a plan

Soul Surfing

It is not to have or to hold
It is not separate; it only unfolds
Hidden it may seem; elusive
Forceful are we; abusive
To listen not with ears
To weep not with tears
Neglected, abandoned or forgotten
Empty, expired — rotten
Rebirthed by breath
A new season's fresh fruit
Silence of the mind
A space so acute
Now the rest can exist
No longer on mute

A Breath Of Self

The sun seemed a bit brighter then
I felt the sparkle it placed amid my eye
L a u g h t e r flooded the breeze
dancing among the trees
bristling my hair along its way by
Effortless exhaustion – not a notice of pain
for if there was any, it wasn't bound by strain
A time that was light, pure, and everlasting – could it be?
Surely, I see – among the same tree,
a mere whiff to return

Authentically Me

3

Moments of Ecstatic Bliss

The harder times to write about. The lesser known magic lost without record. Like the sudden inspiration arriving in an instant and you have forgotten by tomorrow. Sudden revelations in the body inaccessible in days to come. For maybe these sweeping in butterflies of divine truth and beauty are not meant to keep.

A Special Inquiry
Opening To Darkness
Morning Loves Untold
Unleashed

A Special Inquiry

Happiness is ringing
SINGING — radiating through my skin
I've found the lve only dreams provide
I had never thought to inquire

within

Opening To Darkness

The darkest night opened,
across a velvet sky

Surely taken as a token,
the atmosphere stole my pride

As twilight approached,
a certain peace took flight

Carrying me to the moon,
the stars, the cosmos

that night

I rollicked with Orion,
I tangoed with Eros,

Apollo adjourned my crying,
and Athena told me not

to boast

I found love, I found sorrow,
yet with gratitude alike

I could not sleep, for tomorrow,
would fall short of

t o n i g h t

Morning Loves Untold

Morning loves filled my body
With warmth today
Like a dream
Your hand caressed each curve of my being
As if my heart grew lips and told you
Just how to make it work
Silent healer of hurt
The chill ran down my spine
For shaken were my bones
My eyes roll back
And sighs
Shivers to my toes
Next they grip
Eyes grow wide
As the sun kissed your nose
Suspended between reality and dream
Cheeks of salty rose
I'd longed for that sweet release
Skin-to-skin
Tongue-and-cheek
As if your heart grew lips and told
Just how to love in flex and fold
Silence of ocean's deep
Moved as the current sweeps
Grounding sands of blissful gold
Felt beneath our feet
Knees fall shaking and weak
At home amid our rocky reef
Cozy, rosy and
Complete

In morning loves untold...

Unleashed

Focused and beautiful
In meditation
I frolicked with Spirit
And dreamed of
Freedom touched before
Leaping and vibrant
In wilderness
Spirit of free
Passive work
Joyful being
In abundance
Release

4

Patiently Yearning

The desire for healing and impatience of ego.

Reduced Speed Ahead
Curses For A Healer
Fuel Your Own Flame
Healing Gently
A Reason To Stay
The Elemental One
Scavenger Dreams
"Real-Eyes"
A Fear Parable
Alchemy Rising
Perfection
Love Redundancy
A Reminder For Spirit
Struggle Beyond
Warrior Cultivation
Imaginary Ladder
She Leaves
Fluidity

Reduced Speed Ahead

How long has it been?
Weeks, months – six, in fact
Each moment moves faster
Presence, I've lacked
Do not discredit
For there has been progress
But to open three books at once
A mass of lost content
To speed will not arrive you faster
Missing signs along the way
Not quantity, but,
Quality perseveres
If only for a moment
In stillness I lay

"What a beautiful view"

That's what I'll say

Curses For A Healer

Anger – Spite – Hurt ;
from where, I do not detect

The outer shell of a stranger
Detached from which it must protect

Eyes of scorn and patience be none
The deepest breath brings salvation

Caught within emotions unclaimed
Taking upon another's damnation

Darkness floods the light of day
from where remains unknown

Obsessive – Compulsive – Disarray ;
morphing technicolor to drone

I'm reaching for you
Please see me through

If you can hold the fragments
I've found the glue

Fuel Your Own Flame

Those we love, we continue to fix
No matter how broken they become
I, for one, torn and frayed
A time of self-healing assumed
To love one is to love all
A patching tactic for success
Shine bright – shed light
A fortune beheld – no less
Absorbed for an instant – a moment of absence
Then, freed upon return of the breath
A world that promises nothing but change
Provides an uncertain trajectory
To thrive in ambiguity, trusting in unity
Reveals an infinite memory

Depressive Immunity

Healing Gently

Be gentle with her
nurture her and be kind

For change is in the air
she needs a place to unwind

Be gentle with her
do not feel sorrow or have pity

For it will not be long before
she begins a dance with ambiguity

The wound is still fresh but all pain heals

She'll begin to mend her torn seams
her broken heart strings

Tipping with abundance
as the void seals

Carrying along with the flow of the know
the beauty of life

Revealed

A Reason To Stay

To heal is to feel burned
with passion of fire and a ♡ that yearns

To find time alone ignites the flame
a spirit untamed and a ♡ that learns

To listen to the softness
to read text-less words

Is to trust in divine oneness
and illustrate the unheard

The sun continues to warm us
and the wind arrives to play

We are and we have all that we need
to manifest a masterpiece each day

Lessons of vast array

The Elemental One

When I look at you,
I see me —
A familiar flame alighted behind the eyes.
I see myself —
A leaf on the tree.
One of many —
One in the same —
But, somehow,

Unique.

To be humbled is to know unity, interconnectedness and faith. To continue on without concrete understanding — or any promise at all — is to know change. To open the eyes far and wide — acknowledging the past will never return and the future has yet to actualize — to flourish in the present, the only thing that has ever been or ever will be — is to be the flower of the tree.

🙖 Budding, blooming, then falling to rest in the sea. 🙖

Scavenger Dreams

I'll invite a smile to play today
for a smile conveys more than I can say
for the balancing act is not easily done
but a joyous reward awaits this one

❯

Drowning in dreams — luxuriously warming, they enchantingly gleam. Time begins slipping and days become weeks — a passion, an attraction; but then, she weeps. To have all is to have none, a scavenger knows not the likes of fun.

I'll invite a smile to play today, in hopes to entice the love lost along the way.

"Real-Eyes"

Don't abandon her —
for she is you
More than a snippet to capture
Don't abandon her —
touch and love her
A body of the mind's factor
Don't abandon her —
unfairness as the choice is yours
Ungrateful for the gift before
Don't abandon her —
awaken, know and grow her
The struggle brings the cure
a deepened heart

profoundly pure

A Fear Parable

Let go — and be happy about it.

Gee whiz — if I fall, where will I land?

Fear abides by the deepest constraints — what a shame.

A prison of a mind; unrealized.

Illuminated, then, undefined. Lost: a full plate with no context for the carrots. No recognition of beans; because you are still crying over burnt bread.

The present is infinite — so, why live in the past? Craving memories of sorrow — not even happiness to borrow.

Let go — lightheartedly so...

Alchemy Rising

Sunshine
A first of sorts
Springtime
Grass to feed the horse
Letting go
While lighting the torch
Climbing
Above cliffs of self-doubt
United
Realization
Confirmation
Warriors understanding
Difficulty of route

Perfection

Working to find the words
Provides awareness
Of importance
Of presence
Thinking-mind wandering
A thief of the gift
Gift of the moment
All consuming of life
Always concerned
In past or future
Grasping for what
We let slip
A w a y

Love Redundancy

I love to love
To feel, to hold, to shine
I seek this love
I reach out for every kind
Wanting to open
To pour out what has been stowed
The freedom that once flowed
Maybe it's fear
The force which hides
Colors turn gray
Eyes look away
Maybe it's ego
Striving for more
Rattling closed doors
Questioning;
"Just once" more
Tension provides statue
No change, no transform
To release, to let go —
A lull in the storm
Clouds begin clearing
Again the sun will rise —

Finding peace between the turning of the tides.

A Reminder for Spirit

I haven't written in ages
A blocked flow
I haven't let go
Stifled I feel & afraid to show
Transparent as a ghost
Truth gone unnoticed
In order to speak, a voice must grow
Connection defines the courageous
Dimly lit but an eternal born
Will be found upon return
Months have passed
Or just a moment or two
For time, we shall not yearn
T'will only stifle the burn
Glimpsing at the tranquil
Moments of bliss upon the wave
Struggling and wavering within the darkness
but within the self, one cannot cave
A SPIRIT OF BRAVE

Struggle Beyond

Tiresome is the trial
But a means to an endless game
Uncertainty bears residence
Then, it is "I" that remain
A question of better fortune
A fear of choosing regret

Do you recall the motive for voyage?

Of which you are certain,
you will not get?

Hands reaching for any & all
of but an insult to the soul

Begin again;

Yourself, befriend,

Allow your worth to unfold.

Warrior Cultivation

Sometimes when I return, I expect a certain flow. One that rhymes, lines of underlying meaning and implicit messages.

This expectation, this resistance may well inhibit the flow. But sometimes, it spews like a Yellowstone geyser in just the edgy, heady way I desire.

There is a line between <u>force</u> (in desire for a result) and <u>effort at ease</u> (tuning in and finding the self upon a result).

A line between tension and release; <u>battle</u> and <u>surrender</u>.

Perhaps it is here, in both writing and daily life, that we are posed with a trial — the quest, the long-wavering-rocky-endlessly continuing <u>quest for balance</u>.

To progress, one must take forward action — therefore, exerting effort or battling impediments. As I like to think, to progress, one must <u>embody the warrior</u>.

However, to move forward — one must also let go of the heavy weight of <u>prior beliefs</u>: self-doubt, skewed + distorted body image, stale relationships that are no longer fruitful, past expectations of family or loved ones and self-expected results that are not authentic to the higher self.

One must release comfortable habits and possessions that have brought an artificial sense of safety + stability.

Letting go of who I was as a child, as a high-schooler, letting go of my role in "this" relationship or "that" friend group. Letting go of who I chose to be in college when I was societally pressured to decide my purpose.

My life-long venture in a state of disillusioned self-ignorance and utter carelessness; for the person I was scrambling to become, had not yet met the being that I am.

Within the oasis of letting go; a place of surrender, a place of release, exists. A place of granting yourself permission to approve of + fully embody your / our / most authentic self.

Within the freedom of self-acceptance lies true, righteous power. Free from worry and stress, only utter acceptance of the Now can apply. Dwellings upon on the past and anxieties of the future vanish into the healing, grounding + humbling radiance of the present moment.

This unlocks the door to new patterns of thinking — unlocks mind-power that was once consumed by the ego. This release is what gifts to us the true joys in every moment, every interaction.

It bestows the richness, abundance and ability to co-create our lives (individually and eventually collectively) into that which we aspire + were born to create.

The power of being the Creator must begin with separation of the Higher Self from the Ego.

To be aware of the Ego, to observe the Ego, as a separate stream of being in which selfishness, greedy impulses, disconnection from the natural world and superficial thinking spore—is the path to freedom of the Mind.

When the Thinking Mind is no longer ruled and consumed by the Ego › when the Ego is dissolved in the profoundly sobering presence of Consciousness; the relaxed, wide-eyed and clear-minded "I" can live authentically and freely.

To let go is to persevere – to rise from the anxieties of judgement, to let go of the self-concerned ambiguities; to allow space for the spirited, self-teaching, unwavering...

Peaceful warrior within.

Imaginary Ladder

Help

I keep calling out
With no one to help
But myself
Drowning in my own worry
Pools of unforeseen events
That may never exist at all

I've persevered the steps
And climbed a ladder to this place
Only to look down
And wonder if I considered
Where I was climbing to
Or if

I was escaping

Run

Young one
As fast as you can
Go away to college
In a far away land
You'll find something to do
In a year or two
And if you don't

Don't worry
Nobody's got a clue

Pause
Breathe
See

Advertising is not
What lights me up
But pays the bills

Yoga ignites
An eternal flame
But doesn't seem to pay
Until today

Now, there's a way...

She Leaves

Twin flames of similar fuels
Burning on unique paths
But if these paths melded
To trek the same road
The fire could not last
Dampened dreams and
Stifled hearts
If they did not choose to part
A calling to each
Heard by both
Divine intuition
Provides the start
Without a map
But with passionate purpose
A solo journey
Departs

Fluidity

The body is not stiff
The mind is not stiff
Nonresistance
Like springtime,
Waters,
Drizzling rain
Streams trickling
Dew forming
Carving the path;
but gently
Letting go; not forcing,
waiting – receiving
Loving whole; not changing
Accepting, opening to,
The Path

5

Reaching for Solid Ground

The grasping and clinging amid shedding layers inhibiting self-growth in ways of chaotic contentment. The intensity of divinely-timed reshuffling changing everything all at once. Left without a paddle and swept away down stream. The stripped-raw-ness embodied in a familiar grasping rooted in ego's identity while learning the soul's calling is for much more. The karmic ties unbroken and awaiting the self's deciding and wanting in releasing conditioning of egoic expecting, fearing, clinging and hurting.

A Frosty Winter Tale
Emotional Rest
Paper & Scissors
"I'm Here"
Beauty Slaying Beast
Hello?

A Frosty Winter Tale

Twenty-four hours seared
Frosty skies cleared
With a new vision to see
She gasped,
"...was that me?"
As harsh as winter's night
As if bitten by the ice
She casted away her light
In the eclipse of ego & fright
A grasping fear of being alone
An expectation of being left in the cold
She would rather be accepted
For a burst of anger
Than rejected
For her feelings of the other
It was too much a burden to bear
The other, had a real lack
For emotional care
Warmed by a reflection
In the mirror called rejection
She realized, by hiding her heart
They drifted further apart
Common ground lost amid the storm
Self-sabotage of the one once warm
Lay down your mighty shield
My dear

The heart stripped raw
In order to thaw
Warming, again, the soul
The one she left in the cold
And had not realized she blamed
The confused other
For her locked-and-boxed,
Inner-keeping of pain
Truth found, as the veil lifted
From egoic conceal
Her heart had gently shifted
Emerging space to grow & heal
She changed on the inside that day
She had to lose herself before
She walked away
She had not noticed the absence
Filled by another's presence
The void of her inner heart space
Developed when herself she replaced
Inner pools of acceptance begin to rise
A flooding sensation creases her eyes
Love moving both inward and out
Unfamiliar after years in drought
Nostalgia of a younger time
Planted laughter in soul
A voice that she loved
Her loving-self
She remembered
Leaving only a tear
Nothing left to say or hear

Unaware of how far she was gone
Until she heard the inner-song
Frosted by invalidated heartache
She understood why she hid away
She couldn't embody herself, it felt,
Or the other would not stay
Her frosted heart of blue
Could finally relate
An offer of time
And a state
From herself
To contemplate
When assigned to the other
A chilly heart she knew
With release of ego's cover
Awareness inside her grew
Eyes softened
And she discovered
Two kindred playground lovers
Dancing with swords
Shielding their forts
A fantasy of flowery fields
Fell away, one day
Reality harsh in reveal
Though it felt damn good to feel
The release of blame and closure
Allowing her inner soldier
To bow and accept
The war was over

Emotional Rest

Hurt, hurt; hurtinggg

Ouch, my heart
A vice at sternum

And my shell hardened
Then, releasing into hurt

Bathing in emotion
Drinking the potion

A dangerous devotion

Fear overwhelms—
Though knowing there's nothing to fear

Becoming fearful of why I fear

Tap, tap, tap gently
Into the chest

Find treasure while at rest

Paper & Scissors

If the love is true
It will make it through
If the love is not
Growth and development will stop
And either way
It's okay
A flower cannot
Embody a rock
To ask either to alter its beauty
Will surely crush their hearts

"I'm Here"

It's been a many days now
Under the weather +
Over the world
Holding on by vices
Resisting the hurl
Tireless thoughts
Working for rest
Letting go of nothing
Hoping for the best
How many months
Are in a weak
?
Surrender to the moment
Of eternity
Escape in the mind
A prison, no less
Pushing the flow,
Pulling of the know,
...a voice says softly,
"Child, rest."

Beauty Slaying Beast

I never realized how much of a problem it was
Until I imagined you acting the way that I have
No wonder you don't totally trust me
No wonder it's hard to love me
No wonder problems keep cycling
I never separated behavior from the party scene
I never looked at it as problematic rather than normal
Conditioned, for so long, I couldn't even see it

I knew I upset you
I just thought you were up-tight
I didn't see the hurt and pain I was causing
No wonder you never dared to get close
I pushed you away for the distance I thought you created
I was too ego-centric to see it was me
Not aware of how much you cared
Or how tired of caring I made you
I am waking to the nightmare of myself
Always wondering what I needed to do to deserve your love
But I couldn't see
I always had it
Conditionally
Before the condition of acting like a monster
Before I turned into a pattern condition
Now I wonder how attacked you must have felt
My unruly emotions, taken out on you

Created rules for distance
Pushing my own self away
When it was never you
My condition

I am sorry I never created enough consistency for you to trust me
and then, wondered how you could not trust the beautiful
person I am
The beauty of the sea does not meet the darkened beasts
beneath
Until they consume her
Finally, I know
I know, I could've had the love I yearned all along
If I were only taking care of myself first
By neglecting myself, the only person that needs me
I became weak, again and again; headstrong
Wanting you to love me because I could not
I did not see the amount of hurt I carry
Maybe from my past, maybe from my thoughts
I could not grasp what it meant to take care of myself
Finally beginning to see my careless expression
Not caring about what happens, not concerned of safety
I knew damn well I didn't trust myself, so
How the hell could you trust me?

If the beauty was not afraid of the beast
If she were strong enough to wrangle that which controlled her,
and to protect the ones she loves from the wrath of self-
destruction
She would be free to shine
She would be strong

She would be loved
She would no longer ask why
She would be all the things she dreamed of being
The things she wondered why she couldn't be
If only she had loved herself enough first
To stop drowning herself in toxicity
Suddenly it appears, so simple
As if the war was over and the skies had cleared
The imprisoned queen felt the sunshine on her face
Again, for the first time
The darkest beasts scattered with the light of awareness
They were hungry for something to feed on
But here there was none
The queen became curious of her new view
Exploring more beautiful landscapes than before
Honestly, unsure of where she would go next
Walking gracefully her along path
One hand on her belly to ease the uncertainty
One hand to her heart to release the fear
Tracing each curve of her bosom and face
Filling with breath in every place
Coming to know more than a taste
In the love of her own embrace
A new day, a new reign, my dear

Hello?

Dear child
What is it?
You're bursting to flames
What's wrong with you, girl?
Behaving so strange
Sobbing a stream
Bubbling and steaming
Throwing a tantrum
But what is the reason?
Your milk was spilt
Your pencil was broken
Dismissed emotion
Taken as a token
My butterfly died
And it's all my fault
This thing is eating me alive
Crystalized inside
Parasite of empty eyes
But I'm mostly still alive
Unmoved by my
jumps,
heaps,
reaches and
clings

The solitude stings.

6

Divine Intervention

The self beginning to know change is necessary in order for spiritual evolution but also self not-knowing how to bridge the leap. The calling from the most authentic, inner-self gives Spirit permission to soon offer assistance in releasing the grip of identity and fear of failure. The asking of Spirit to help the self let go and flow. The magically occurring ways that life falls apart so beautifully that the Soul recalls purpose. The known paths of darkness suddenly changing from "peace-of-mind" to interpersonal warfare and warning. The guides of Love and Light arriving, offering support and connection and the self is shaken.

Budding With Source
I Love You, Child
Rewiring The Ocean
Sonshine

Budding With Source

Divine says to the bud,
You are blessed, little one
You are built of love + light
So tightly packed into your heart;
The guard around keep tight
You want to be free, little one
So, let the heart be
Have tea with your fears
And welcome your tears;
Softening the eyes to see
I am cheering for you, little one
When you are cheering too
It is what you sow—
That which you will reap
So, come with me, little one
No need to dress or shower
This is not a school test,
Or competition with the rest,
but effortless...
is the unseen bloom of the flower.

I Love You, Child

I had a thought come to mind
Placed if you will —
On navigating the growth
As both mother and child
Could one be named without the other?
The teacher and
The one who is taught
A caregiver could not exist
Without the one
On the cot
To embody both
The self who learns and
The self who guides
Nurturing growth
Compassion evoked —
Pulsating between
Aged wisdom and
Adolescent tides
A crash of a wave
All structures shatter below
Falling adrift
Amid the rift
Weeps the child alone
Eyes of helplessness open to see
Calmness upon the crest
Reminded by love

As if consoled by a mother
Held in the child's chest
When compassion arises in
The heart of this child
The storm of the self
Subsides
Instead of punishing
And resisting the waves
Easing into a mother's eye
Embodying both child and
The mother amid
The turning
Of the tides

Rewiring The Ocean

She began again
To fill the holes which poured
Each time something different
Along the quilted shore
When I pause between the tides
I hear those silver bubbles rise
And each one has to say
The same thing in a different way
Life's between the motions
The choices, thoughts and beliefs
There in the space between
Pathways for bubbles develop
And once you hear
And pause to listen
You'll know you were not so lost
Amid layers of murk and muddy waters
Breathe in to find the light
Fill your spaces
Envision these places
Love as a dream could be
Healing and held
Just being "me?"
He doesn't mean to hurt you
He would love you if he could
There may be weights heavy to bear
If only you understood

Sonshine

The sun shines for moments
Before it conceals;
The warmth
Which remains within us
His gift revealed
For once or for always
Only by our choice to feel

7

Dark Night of the Soul

The dark night of the soul emerging, encapsulating, engulfing and cultivating the deepest fears and attachments of the ego. The actualizing of attachments lost left nothing to attach to and so, fear released and blockages to true self worth were removed in a sweet moment's pain. The seedling returning to darkness beneath the soil after a first flowering and falling again to remember where it is to begin blooming anew. The lesser known planes of higher alignment shifting and recalibrating the journey as the self comes closer to soul purpose. The inner-knowing-ness that all is well and beheld by the Universe. The darkest times feeling like abandonment, fabrication, damnation, self-reflection, deception, separation and hardening of the trusting heart. The questioning of Spirit in the solace of solitude.

Oceanic Love
Distant Hurting
Frozen Toes
Entanglement
Fear of the Unknown

Oceanic Love

If you want to heat her up
Words of love, you'll say

Remind her of her beauty
And promise that you'll stay

If you're here to love her
With a heart of gold

All on your own
Think twice

Take caution at the break of day
And a memo of advice:

You'll sometimes have her row your boat
Somewhere aimless along the coast

She's an ancient queen atop the sea
But she doesn't hope to journey alone

An ancient queen
What does that mean?

You can find a clue in *blue*

Free as the wind
She wanders

Carrying armor along her side

Not in fear of battles onward
In preparation for the tides

Worried for the innards of others
When blame became her truth

But even at her warmest
You could not love her blue

A queen of one
No more to come

Not ever alone
An embodied throne

Floating along the breeze
She walks away
Better luck another day

Seashells bring her home.

Distant Hurting

I'm sorry
And embarrassed
For these moments
To say
I allowed a past version of my coping
To rule and complain
I noticed the negativity
I felt child-like and aloof
I felt drained
And then, I said,

"Are you not seeing, hearing and abstaining?
Touching, feeling and perceiving?
The beauty in all living beings"

Would you like to choose beautiful, loving presence instead?
Would you like to focus your energy more
On following another thread?
Rather than slyly (or not so) slinging
Comments about a "poor me"
And stinging

Do you choose to neither slave
nor siege
Over others,
and,

Parallel leaves...

You find your own compulsive thinking
To be the deceiving ego (mind)

Not a thought of blinking
Or remaining kind

We call this anxiety of the mind

Beware the darkness of blind.

Frozen Toes

I long to find the exquisite inspiration to write
To write out a clear understanding
Of what I have been
In plight
After writing a sentence
I fumbled through ideas
Left in a triage
And losing sight
Of how I thought I felt
No words felt real
A divine blockage
Between dis-ease and mis-understanding
And what this soul feels
For myself and of others
I cannot unfold
Do I feel ever cold
Perhaps the toe tips are numb
The outlines of mold
Though numb and of mold,
The temperature brings awareness
As a mirror, I'm told...
When I touch
The opposite toes
Though frozen and numb
I find,
A soft mirror

One that resembles the hum
Perhaps that's it,
These toes would not know
But only before, how cold they once were
If not contrasted by the warmth of the other
Awareness given from a mirrorly brother
Like I would not hear
The spoken last sentence
I feared
My tone so stunningly harsh and bold
If not contrasted by the warmth of my mother.

Fear of the Unknown

the world has been sad
i am coming to know
after years, i spent
pretending
it wasn't so
when darkness is faced
it can feel surreal
like it shouldn't be
the way that it is
a broken seal
perhaps the breakage
perhaps the bond
lies in the attachment
in the way we interpret
our world
death
as it seems
a transitioning
not an ending
gateway to infinity
but
why does it ache my heart so?
why does it pull our hearts together
in common
misunderstanding
the clinging

to right and wrong
to only happy songs
to fear of the unknown
to what we've "known"
aho

8

Spiritual Decree

The beginning building of pathways between Self and Source. The release of outside, egoic expectations of self. The release of former identities to create space for inhabiting the Soul's truth. The unfortunate occurrences becoming the most fortunate opportunities. The deepest desires begin actualizing as perspective on the dark night transforms from punishment to development.

Reality Infinity
Softening
Spatial
Secrets of the Light

Reality Infinity

Universe! I want to know you
To feel your love and hear your truth
To live more than exist and to know every last bit
I think that's probably not common in this reality
So filled with buzz, fuzz & distortions of our own doing
but
Shouldn't that be the hidden, divine beauty?
The co-creation:
the gift of opportunity
of free-will
of learning + growth
How beautiful would it be
If we were mere observers of an outside project?
Pretty, I suppose, it would be
But Divine!
Is when the words flow into rhymes
When we lose track of time
And fall from the vine
Amid that mysterious state of flow
When we forget what we "know"
We surrender the force, and
We receive as we let go
We see the brightness line
The horizon
As one day sets itself
Each cloud, a soft silver (or golden) lining

Beautiful, only it is,
When we are not angered by snow
You know, since we do not know
Could it be simple to not
Expect where we go?
If we do not know
Just how we Earthed here
So many cataclysmic years ago
Why must we scurry to and fro
Blaming by thought
Angered if lost?
Could it be, these diversions
Are meant to set us free?
A door to the unknown
Answers be shown
If only we'll smile
and stay for awhile
Breathing in wild air
And breathe out to share
Love pours
In a drink
From the infinite sea
Infinity

Softening

Love given to others
Parallels love given to self
Sometimes grounded
Vulnerable and honest
Sometimes fearful
Manipulative and shielded
Sometimes unaware
Sometimes uncertain
Sometimes not love at all
But more than before
Opening to
A heart-opening
A breakthrough
Intention to love freely
Courageously and curiously
Genuinely and boldly
To share this love with others
In the same regard as self
Open and free
And lovable
Glimpsing more often
Other as me
I as other
Letting go
Releasing boundaries
Expanding into oneness
Into loving being

Spatial

By the way, I love this feeling
Of floating on the edge
Flirting
With death?
With closeness?
The place between
Which allows
Myself to be seen
By myself
Without doubt
Full of surrender
In being
In loving danger
Close, I feel

Secrets of the Light

If you will agree to write
The Universe agrees with you
To pass through you
The whistling winds
Inspiring you
Made of you

Secrets of the Light

9

Releasing Karmic Ties

The awareness, reflection, understanding and integration forming of childhood conditioning, toxic romantic patterning and self-sabotage. The accepting of how the path unfolded before providing insight for future direction. The surrender of fear and decision to grow after many cycles arriving. When the Self is accepting truth, a willingness to embody and embrace true self and soul purpose as a spiritual warrior and without attaching to anything. The release of karmic ties when action is taken in truth and devotion.

Peaceful Seeing
Yin & Yang
Polarization
Deciding
False Memories
Password
Scales

Peaceful Seeing

I've been awake for two hours now
While he sleeps soundly, and,
It's 8:40 in the morning
The stillness speaks
Chirps on the wind
Kitty in the window again
Warm tea for me
As I wonder what he dreams
A bit numb or perhaps still
Happily sipping tea
Without a story to tell

Yin & Yang

I had a sudden realization
I loved to be me
The little girl
Of vibrant colors
Of loving, sensual spirit
The little boy
Who had cool clothes
One of the boys
We are the same one
Let us be us again
And let us love again
Without separation
In balance instead
Of polarity

Polarization

You ride the waves of my mind
Sweeping me away
Throughout the day
Everyday
You surf the perfect line
But, you might, in time
Just pop in to say
That I've been sailing through too
The eye of the storm of truth
Casting to the horizon
Your line
Careful, to not,
Look directly into the sun
For a lost voyage is not fun
For anyone...
A risk of being blinded
And swept away
They say
For once, by the heart,
Who's promising to stay
Keeping the logical heart
At bay

Deciding

To the end of a chapter
The last let go
Smile and you'll know
And you'll grow
Spaciousness
Emptiness
Embrace it
But you have to first decide
That you've made up your mind
Habit will urge you to comfort
To seek love in places known before
But remember!
And a bit more...
You are here!
You decided...
That place once known
Doesn't exist anymore
Imagined
Expected
Dare I say
Never existed at all
Be done with the madness
Be done with the longing
Be done with the lying
And saying
To yourself
"Trying"

False Memories

Prolonged ending of a chapter
Of love and laughter
Of emotional disaster
Longing thereafter
Recall and you'll know
It's time to grow
And you'll find
Spaciousness
Emptiness
Of the sacred kind
But you have to decide
You've made up your mind
When it tugs at your pride
And you feel misaligned
Remember why
You closed the door
Again, you are here
As many times before
This place of loss, in fear,
Does not (truly) exist
Imagined
Enthralled
Love gone amiss
And overly involved
Years spent knocking, banging,
Against the heart's great wall

It's your choice to make
Or your heart to break
Again —
Once and for all
You can see it, now,
Stand tall, girl,
and
Evolve

Password

As I tell myself
About this *innerfruit*
I feel the darker layers in bloom
As if just in time
To cut me from the vine
But this time
I'm too sure
I've seen you before
Layers of darkness and decay
I ignore
For there is no other way to be
You can't hide and you can't flee
Until you shake, the once upon
You locked
Door

Scales

Suddenly waves of people crash in
Whom I thought I'd lost but
Maybe didn't

Time does not reciprocate
Momentary feelings
In an instant

Yet,
Love flows 'round
Here ; There

And back again

On a balanced plane
An even keel
We wish
Balance found
Reflections abound
With patience

Divine timing's kiss

10

Expanding Into Growth

The journey of love for everything. The rootedness in being. The book ending in the middle of the story. The book of continually evolving, releasing and opening. The book of bending and breaking, loving and hating, understanding and absorption. The book of learning the balancing of retracting and expanding.

Grace

Lioness Training

Adrift

Chipper

Close To hOMe

42

Believe To Receive

Grace

Real abundance
Wholesome abundance
Tenfold abundance

All-encompassing
Multidimensional
Abundance

Intentional
Graceful
Focused

Manifestation
Suddenly
All at once

Realized
Remember
Flow

Forward
Onward
Go

Lioness Training

This story
A script
A hundred years old
Ending the same
Every time told

Be open in mind
Watchful of emotion
Stern in decision
Let go in devotion

A life of choice
A life of worth
When cycles are broken

Be serious
Be wise
You know how to devise

Seek your insides
Release comparison
Competitive pride

Work is required
For freedom in mind
And it must come from you

Others have not
Your contract to truth

It becomes clear
Patterns of fear
It wasn't your heart
He was after
My dear

Leaving you here
This hundredth year

Exhaustion releases
A caged-up beast

Surrender in healing
Set yourself free

Let your voice rise
Let your spirit fly
Begin to ROAR
And revive

Power and beauty
Loving integrity

When you change your mind
You change your trajectory

Promise to your heart
Honor your part

And decide

A shame would it be
To cycle around
Year hundred and three

Karma and hurt
Uncover your worth

Love and arise
To your surprise

Cycles release
Enters Divine

Morning mountains
Moving into and through

The freedom
You are seeking

Releasing
Karmic ties
Family history

ROAR—
To embody

ROAR—
To believe

Your ROAR is your movement
Closer to your dreams

A drumming inspiration
A sudden manifestation

A path now cleared
In clarity and precision

Softly encouraged
To make a decision

And again,
She ROARED

These ambitions of yours

Remember before?

Set aside to simmer

Fear of being seen
To you; they are delivered

To you; most keen
You have gifts to explore

Activations of dreams
You are rewarded

Will you receive?

Self accepts, and,
Spirit stills

Gracious

Calling unfolds, and,
Heart opens

Courageous

The flame is ignited
To make you aware

Of your dreams, your gifts,
What you came here to share

Embodiment of the lion
Fuels the collective fire

Keep humble and kind
In heart be aligned

Pathways of Divine
You will find

To your innermost desires

When you surrender

Your time

Adrift

Isn't it amazing
I am my own best friend
And at the same time
Hide away all day
You don't truly know
The value of my smile
And
You don't truly know
The value in what I say
But nor do I
Sometimes, I think
Because not yet can even I see
When the cycle sweeps me
If lessons I've learned
If much I've grown
If there is one thing I know
It flows and as I let go
And you'll find me
Carried gently
Back out to the troughs of the sea
With a familiar horizon
Just a returning visitor
Seeking to understand
And perhaps find
Remains of every lost voyage
A lingering detail of why

I come back, again, to find
Each shipwreck of mine
To find completion is to find resolution
To resolve is to move past
But I like the view
From the crest of epiphany
So today, I'll relax as I float on my back
Along shores of pondering
Grounding found only at a distance
For an instant
I prefer the water anyway
Forever spelunking
Perhaps
Forever diving into
Unbeknown depths
Forever seeking the hiding
Shadowy crevasses of mind
The forbidden territory
The common history
Prodding at the wound
When I could've just let it be
And, sudden tossing
And, again tangling
This is great fun in truth
For me, you see...
Tide carries me
As it has for all of time
I realize
An oddly comforting feeling
Solaced by aloneness
In ever expanse of oceans wide

A notion of freedom of self
Drifting and returning
Freely and alively
Amazing is the break of the wave
Just before dawn
I understand

Chipper

To be cheerful
Can we recall for always?
The flip of a switch
Accessible at all times
Infinitive energy
In times of depletion
A low burning smolder
Can we gift ourselves rest?
And burn brighter
When we're older?
A nap for the mind
A rest for the soul
Instead of
A deeper dug hole
A smile we bring
We dance
We sing
And we rest
By existing

Close To hOMe

A walnutty, chocolatey treat
Is a 4 o'clock cup of joe
A misty 50-degree breeze
Strolling cozy and refreshed
Noticing the numbers
Vibrance of colors
The homes gone unnoticed
The passing faces slow
A stream so close to home
Offering ; providing
Hope

42

If 42 is the answer
If the choice is yours
Which creation would you dream of?
Where would you explore?
If there was no meaning
Beyond you ; no more
If you were the decider
How far would you go?
Since limit does not exist
And it is whatever you want it to be
Will you dance with me into infinity?
Or fearfully close the door?

Please no — let's go!

Believe To Receive

The reason you're not receiving
Is not lack of efficacy
The reason you stand needing
Is because you're not believing
If you say to your heart
This may not be my part
Instead of confiding
From the start
Your story changes
From your control and desire
To victim burned
By the mis-intended fire
Hear it? B E L I E V E IT.
Feel it? B E IT.

Hold in your heart the truth of your soul with all the grip of
your bones and pleasureful growns — for this is yours . . .

A c t . a s . s o !

11

Self-Recognition

The ignition of self. The setting afire. The sudden integration of gifts and clarity of path. The motivation to move forward in mere authenticity and trust. The knowingness. The paving of the road. The fulfillment of self and dreams. The love of Self and Source. The time arriving when it is no longer bearable to trek another path in pursuit of expectations, obligations, shoulds and shouldn'ts. The realization of infinite potentiality found in Ether. The beginning to lovingly join forces with nature. The manifesting. The dreams come true. The YOU.

The Practice
Vessels of Understanding
WRITE ON
Illuminated Soul
Winged Warriors

The Practice

I feel at home in this body
I am coming to know
The way it moves
Fluid in the air
Longing to grow
A seed once planted
Approaching a harvest
A harvest of ripples spiraling onward
With many more seeds to sow

Vessels of Understanding

Sometimes wine
Coats my desires
In all things I need
To hear
The away-ness
Of my heart
Fading
I see truly
What I might be
And what you might be
Do you say wine is wrong?
For me
I like to disagree
Who would've felt
What I feel, tonight,
Had it not been for
The red river
That carried me

WRITE ON

SO! I CHOOSE to write
For the expression of LOVE + LIGHT
Brings such delight
There remains
No plight
SO! I TRUST the transition
And the path less traveled
But greatly rewarded in scenery
And greenery
Allotting the space for
G . R . O . W . T . H
INTO! The most high embodiment of self
The land of nonresistance
The truth of effortless expression
And existence
And cheerfulness
YOGANANDA; I pray
And thank you; I say

Illuminated Soul

He took my breath away
My heart poured
My words jumbled
And I couldn't tell
If he's married; or if,
and, he's into me
But his eyes lit up
Like mine and
To gaze in and
Around him
Felt divine
From another life
It felt
I'm supposed to know
Dearest elf

Winged Warriors

Angels do hurt
And they do cry
Wings become tired
Their eyes won't lie
They sometimes get injured
Protectors of all places and time
In endless concern and love
Compassionately inclined
And when they are broken
When they, the healers, need healing
When the protectors need protection
Still they are
Protecting and healing
Children of Divine
Like all of Creation
In dark hours, they return home
To the vital Source
Some call "OM"
Beheld they are
Mother and Father
Medicine and Movement
Support each other
Though Angels see darkness
Forever Holders of the Light
Forever Holders of the Space
Even amid, the Darkest Night

Their revitalization lies
In the wake of the morning sun
The Light at the end of the tunnel
Realizes itself
It has illuminated
Shining every last lumen
When exhaustion bears witness
An internal transmission
Breaks free the Darkest Hour
Embodiment becoming
High Priestess of One
When the player of the game
Recalls its purpose of fun
When the worker of the purpose
Recalls the Higher One
When the piece becomes the puzzle
And the land becomes the sea
When the heart becomes the caretaker
The "you" becomes the "me"
The Soul becomes The Freed
The Light becomes Thee
The Pleasure of the Endeavor,
Then, moves about
Peacefully
And joyfully
The Kingdom Comes
Kingdom of One
Angels do hurt
And they rise again
Among supernova skies
Of cataclysm

Of Holy Reign
Within the planes of pains
Deeper healing engrained
Greater plains of peace
Foresight be seen
Wild beauty untamed
If it weren't for the battlefield
Warrior wouldn't look to the sky
Dreamer wouldn't dream
Angels wouldn't cry
Endless supplies of love
Be left unrecognized
For deep within the turning of the tides
The Guru abides
And the Guru emerges
Somewhat
Surprised

12

The Light

The call received. The answer Source has patiently and excitedly awaited. The attunement. The blending with the AUM. The living as one. The ringing of the ears that replaces the ringing of the phone. The inspirations alive. The freely, openly sharing of dialogue without fear or hesitation and rooted in integrity. The impeccable word. The purpose, path and mission embodied in self-healing, ancestral healing, global healing and universal healing. The sending of ahimsa to all beings everywhere. The love, the light, the oneness, the strife, the battle, the fun, the glory of the sun, the walking, the living, the here and the now.

The unfolding path of trust, truth, wisdom, authenticity, selflessness, integration and completion - guided by Loving Source, Loving Creator, Loving Divine Feminine, Loving Divine Masculine, Loving Gaia, Loving Omnipresent Intelligence and Loving Self - as the incredibly important and seemingly insignificant speck of sand that completes the whole of creation.

The realized integration of Creation, Creator and Co-Creation. The ever-so-freaking-present, loving, vitalizing, nourishing, necessary and alive exchange of love between Source and Self. The beheld. The romanticized feeling of "what if there is a God and what if God loves me unconditionally" known, experienced and embodied as truth. The sun that warms the month of February.

The synchronicities that blossom new and genuine undertakings. The giving of the light, the truth, the wisdom, the wind, the honor, the healing, the compass, the direction, the freedom, the imperfect perfection, the surrender, the listening ear and the courage that opens doors and creates worlds.

The embodiment of gifts and perpetuation of purpose.

When life becomes a grand, relaxed expression of wild, sexy, raw and creative energy. When the Ether becomes the canvas. When the mind partners with the soul. When the heart swings the doors open so freely that hinges fall away and love invites it all to play.

When the heart no longer retreats to the shell. When the heart becomes so big it cannot possibly be contained in a single, fleshy body. When the heart is realized. When the heart sings. When the heart brings. Grounded, rooted, certain, present, refined intention to each breath, word and action.

And the fun! The blissfulness of living in pure enjoyment... found in the seam between reality and the dream. Coming to be... living in ever completion. When the heart realizes, this is just the beginning...

Shifting Perspective
Wright Creative
Healing Art of Flow
Worlds

Shifting Perspective

My dreams are coming true
All at once but in divine time
I am overwhelmed with gratitude
So much that I can hardly feel
I am so grateful universe
I shine to you my truth
I am dancing in the wonder of
When the shift happened
I embrace this gift from you
Thank you so much universe
I love you so much
Let us dance in the wonder together
& never look back

Wright Creative

Wright Creative
It's write before my eyes
Now I let go of fearful ego
Now I decide
This is what I'm going to do
In divine rhyme I'll bloom
With Creator at my roots
And manifestation in hand
Not so much divine plan
But instead,
Choosing where I stand
In tandem we arrive
In the promised land

Healing Art of Flow

Voice healing
Creation flowing
Inner-knowing
On fire

Releasing feeling
Feelings releasing
Tasting shedding
Of ego

When truth looked in
The eye and
Feeling whatever
Feeling arises

Cycles completing
New records
Transcribing
Endings befriend me today

I've made peace with
The one who needed the healing and the love
When I'd given it all away

The harnessing of a self-hug
Gently kiss this face, whispering,
"A new morning"

Words no longer constrict my throat
Or ache away in my bones
Openly speaking truth

Throw me on the pillows
Softening the throne
A new moon

For a play-date with a new way
New timelines emerging
Aho

In learning

The art of flow

Worlds

Sun peeks through the clouds
Sharing a message
With me; with us
Alike

These breezy,
Delicious, fall afternoons
Give us permission
To radiate our warmth freely

Embrace those chosen days
When your sacred and gifted rays
Penetrate the cloudy weather
Around you

When your light breaks through
And infiltrates the world around you
With life force energy
Giving healing

Use that nourishing nectar of the gods
Which resides within you
And within the core
Of all things

When you can peek through
The clouds around you
For those around you
Shine

Share those subtle yet
Rippling spectrums of vibrant color
That which emanate from you and are
The truest expression of you

And of others too; it will inspire them
The embedded and engrained
Beauty that is
Nature

Share your truest magnificence
When you can
Please do
Flow with this energy

Flow it through you freely
Flow it through you easily
And it will, if you choose it to,
Every day

It flows and it speaks to you
In unique ways
And to others
In their own respected way

It's essence remains true
Hold this light within you
Rain or shine
Hold it dear

The ship does not man the ocean
We must dance with waves of motion
And move in grace always
And remember

Darkness precedes the dawn
The light and dark are one
Dark and light are but an illusion
For the sun is never objectively gone

For sunset occurs as we turn inward
It is the beauty of balance
And knowingness
Nothing is permanent

Recall that, as we turn in,
The sun shines on in the dark
The duality of life
Let it ground you

"Life and death"
"Right and wrong"
"Beginnings and endings"
From which you never depart from

You are never separate from
The innermost spirit of all things
You and the all
Are one

Singular experiences represent
A focal point of all creation to be shown
"One" is a segment of "the all"
Trust your reflections

Live freely
Live fully
Do not judge
Your darkness

When we remember we are both
Of light and of dark
The double standard falls away
And we shine

When we embrace the flux between
What we might call
"Good and bad"
"Right and wrong"

We allow ourselves to be
We allow ourselves to live fully
To be who we truly are
And give credit to our feelings

Unique in each moment
Renewed
Give way to resisting feeling
Our darkness

Born from the light
And equally there is dark
We cannot go wrong
When we live fully

We must find embrace
Of how that we are
And express ourselves
Honestly

From the heart of our experiences
We find who we truly are
Or who we might be
When we embody the balance
Of infinity

We live in a balanced
Double-helix of life
It is just so
There are always both

It is the nature of our physical plane
Our reality on Earth exists of
Equal and opposites
Alike

We are physical and spiritual beings
Emotional and thinking beings
We are both understood and mysterious
Dichotomy; humanity

We are ever-changing but slowly
Our species is constantly evolving
Both physically and consciously
It is our journey

Yet, we are masterpieces unfinished
Works of art and in-progress
In all of our archaic, polarized and
Creative states

We are divine
We live within
A dualistic and intrinsic
Double-helix of life

It could not be any other way
We are embedded
In a matrix, some might say,
An illusion of separation

From one another
And from God
But the illusion is
Fundamental

It becomes essential
To our human experience
To experience both sides
Along our journey to enlightenment

The illusion and disillusion
Provides a human perspective
A lens for which God
Peers through

To experience

The battlefields
Of heart and ego
Of success and failure
And we rise again

Both are necessary and
Fundamentally pure
So that we may eventually see
Clearly

That one cannot exist
Without the other
Always in motion
Tides in turning

This is our nature
And nothing is "wrong"
We live in worlds of duality

We do it heartfully

Flow with your experiences
Let go of right and wrong
Release your polarities
Believe in the higher beyond

And as you do
A feeling may be recalled
Of it all just "is"
It "is what it is"

It is "what has been" created

As we continue on together
Collectively manifesting our thoughts
Let us find ourselves as perfect integrations
We move gracefully

It will be important to
"Mind our minds" along the way
And consciously create
Our thoughts

For thoughts become things
And I think this is our work
To intend the lives we know we deserve
To rise above all that is not pure

To become specific upon the content
To design the context of our dreams
To intend the experiences we deeply wish for
And to pray for love once more

May we keep unconditional love in mind

As we allow there to be peace between
The turning of each tide and the changes of
Each day into each night

Embrace the sunshine
Embrace the storms
Allow there to be change
Allow it to transform

Give honor to your heart's truth
Be aware of becoming "the norm"
On the other side of "you and I"
We rise

Now is the time
For humanity to realize
The flow of the tides
Earth into sky

May we integrate the "divide"
Of life and of mind
Of self and of divine
Naturally

Sing your heart's song
Uncover your sweetness
You subconsciously yearn for
It is all but a dream anyway

Your path unfolds
You find clarity of mind
It comes when you shine, baby,
Shine

Remember
Who you are
And choose
Peace

Let others not sway you
In troubling times
Intuition guides
You already do know

The truths you seek
Are available
To you
Inside

conclusion

The spiritual unfolding and harvesting of a 20-something-year-old's *innerfruit*. Including many moons of life purpose cycling and nurturing self-awareness, self-healing, self-forgiveness, divine connection, integration of purpose, embodiment of self and courageousness carried along the path to truth. Including the shifting from self-healing to universal-healing. From student to teacher. From irresponsible to embodied vessel. From passive to active. From talking to doing. We are reminded with every breath, in every moment of every day. Insights derived from yogic teachings and learnings rooted in the spiritual path of ascension. A series of growing pains, vibrant awakenings and the whiplash found between. Ripped raw and real transformed into graceful and present. When we are honest and see ourselves precisely where and how we are, we are able to see the invisible barricades our darkness places around our inner-fruits. Inner-fruits of purpose, the "why am I here" question's answer, the calling, the no-brainer once we can clearly see what, who and where we truly are. What we are capable of and how capable we are. Of anything. Of anything. Of anything. I say this to you, dear child, to assure you it is safe to know your darkness, it is safe to embody your healing in all its messiness, it is safe for you to grow and see vibrant emissions of Divine all around you and I tell you, dear child, you have been planted to bloom again anew and you are - in the most extravagant version of you. This version is the path to your righteousness and if you follow it, you begin the most fulfilling journey humanly possible to experience. You will sway and you will stray but dear child, that's okay - know that you will be carried through the muck by the Source Energy all around you. The sound of AUM meets your ears, the sparkle in each eye reminds you, the rushing sensation which guides you, the concurrent synchronicities speeding up and suddenly halt.

Halt; Open your eyes to see.
Breathe; Remind yourself daily.
Feel; Inwardly, outwardly and beyondly.
Recall; Reality thrives when in alignment.
Align; Yourself energetically with aim for Truth.

And you create with Creator in the lucid, fluid and constantly-changing field of experience. You create e v e r y t h i n g you think. All thoughts move onward. Bring your focus to love and Divine Purpose and you will find your way. Bring your heart forward to be open, expansive, unconditional and courageous and you will find your strength. Trust in your experience and your study, know Source as Self and Self as Source, tread easily and travel lightly and you come closer. Embody every movement - emotional, mental and physical. And to unlock the key, reside in compassion, truth and positivity. You heal. You heal your ancestors. You heal your future. You heal others. You heal the planet. You heal the universe when you stand in your power. And how?

Ground.
Connect.
Release.
Bless.
Intend.
Know.
Love.

And do not question your certainty. You are far more powerful than you could comprehend and you are far more gentle than the "love" you let in. Let your shackles fall as you break through, wild thing. Drink up every rush of divinity. Embody the sexiest feeling to you. For these sensations are made of the energy that creates worlds and when you release your shackles, this manifestive energy comes of access to you. And when you choose to love, heal and grow no-matter-what, your very most *innerfruit* reveals. Take your courage with you. Your heart is your loving shield. Shine your innermost light forward and compass yourself along the path to purpose. You already have the answers; they appear as you peel.

INNERFRUIT (n.)

The place inside the chest, similar to the heart - holding life purpose and design of your being. The container of dreams (or seeds) waiting for you to plant them - they are awaiting the permission from *you* and acceptance of you to begin their germination. The *essence of you* held within your core - the core of you left pure, sacred and unmuddled by external forces, experiences and projections of the world. The *truest* you, found here. When you trust yourself, when you allow your truest self to be - you will begin. One must be in love, in acceptance with the matter of *Who You Truly Are* and when you are, these fruits begin to ripen. It is what you are here to do. It is how you are here to be. Your quirks, your calls, your strengths - they reside in this *essence of you*. Be strong, be unwavering, be trusting that Who You Are is beautiful and Who You Are *Supposed* to Be. Even through the messiness, even through the troubled times, know that *You Are Healing*. Know that healing is intimately entangled with this process of *Returning Home*. Returning home to *you*.

about the author

Erin was born in Maine to her loving parents, Dawn Woodward and Dean Crowley. Erin moved from Coastal Maine to Cincinnati, Ohio where she studied Advertising and Public Relations at Xavier University, a Jesuit-Catholic university. It was here where her passion ignited within the studies of Theology and spirituality. Erin found interest in yogic studies when she stumbled in the woods one day and was led by a new friend to the doors of VITALITY Cincinnati and became certified to teach yoga and meditation in 2015. VITALITY in later years catalyzed the existence of many poems included here and assisted by publishing this very book. Erin worked in digital media and taught yoga in the community of Cincinnati for several years before moving to Asheville, North Carolina in 2019.

In Asheville, Erin found further meaning in life through surprisingly losing a "dream job" and began to follow a truer heart. Erin started a freelance website business, worked at REI and led yoga hikes along Appalachian Mountain peaks and waterfalls. In Asheville, Erin's writing also cascaded. It was here where she decided to publish her past near-decade of poetry which was written without the intent of ever sharing with anyone. This changed when innerfruit started to compile itself. The concept of chapters and the apparent arrangement of life phases presented itself to her in a metaphysical way. A feeling of knowing, or of "coming-through," encouraged her to sit, write and begin. Thank you pandemic of 2020 for allowing the space and time to do so. Four years later, here we are. Erin is currently 31-years-old and resides in her home state of Maine once again, this time, just outside of the beautiful Acadia National Park in Ellsworth.

On a new journey due to the utterly surprising and transformational nature of life, let this be a testament to us all - to let us truly let go when we are asked to. Let us graciously let go of what was to allow what is now. In 2023, Erin became certified as a Usui Reiki Master Teacher through the school of Vernita Leins at the QiGong Studio in Bangor. From 2021-2024, Erin worked as a professional in providing behavioral health services to children with autism, ADHD, trauma and other special needs in a local residential setting - another unexpected and now coming to be understood adventure. Erin currently works as a gardener on Mount Desert Island and is enjoying a summer's return to a more creatively-charged existence. It is important to find both what you are good at and what is good for you. A new journey in Waldorf education begins this coming Fall.

Thank you for existing. Thank you for being you. Thank you for following your path. Thank you for being here. Thank you for being a vatron. Thank you for spending time with these words. Blessed may you be always.

"The heart is a place where the body and soul meet. Listen to yours. It loves you, too."

- innerfruit

about VITALITY

VITALITY is a circle of friends welcoming all, awakening each other, and reminding each other that we are Whole. Our affordable self-care programs invite everyone to move, to breathe, to rest, to contemplate, to grow...wherever each person begins their self-care journey, wherever and however they want to become.

donation-based drop-in classes...
in person & via Zoom

affordable trainings

individual sessions

volunteer opportunities

vitalitycincinnati.org

VITALITY
buzz, bliss + books

publishing books from VITALITY's circle of friends
inspiring love, creativity, + possibility

vitalitybuzz.org